The Christ Centered Marriage

A Bible study seeking the truth about love and marriage the way God intended

Barbara Marcella

The Christ-Centered Marriage: A Bible study seeking the truth about love and marriage the way God intended

ISBN: 979-8-9894729-0-1 (Paperback Edition)

1st edition, 2023

Cover Design and Interior Illustrations: Daniel Zoino

Cover Handlettering by Letteralle Studios. Cover Font by Flavortype.

To the One who knew me, loved me, and saved me in spite of my sins and flaws, my Lord and Savior Jesus Christ. Everything I am, have, and do—I owe it all to You.

To my husband Danilo, you are a blessing I never expected but the Lord knew I needed. Thank you for your relentless love and for being the kind of man I prayed would someday marry. I love you, forever and always.

Thank you to my little brother and one of my best friends, Danny, for your patience, wisdom, artistic talent, and all of your help in bringing this devotional to life. I couldn't have done it without you, love you!

Two are better than one; because they have a good reward for their labour. ~Ecclesiastes 4:9

Table of Contents

Introduction

Hi! I'm so excited that you are here to learn, grow, and dive deeper into God's word. The beauty and purity of marriage have been under attack since the day sin entered the world. Through music, movies, TV shows, books—you name it—the media is constantly leading society to pervert the original design God intended for marriage.

As a culture, we spend a whole lot of time and money preparing for wedding days. The flowers, the dress, the cake, the venue, the photography—the list goes on and on. Rightfully so, because it is truly a monumental day (I photographed weddings for quite some time and absolutely loved planning every second and detail of my own), but I'm afraid we spend virtually no time preparing for what comes after and is to be far longer and more important: marriage.

This devotional was inspired after making a simple study for a friend before her own wedding. The topic tugged at my heart, and I thought it would be helpful for other women to dive into it as well. And so, after much prayer and Bible study, I have put together this devotional so that others may learn the truth about marriage and what God intended for it. Who better to learn from than the very One who created it, right? So let's go straight to the source: God's word, and learn what He has to say about it.

If you are a woman who is married, about to get married, or hoping to get married someday, I hope this study blesses you and gives you peace about God's good and perfect design for marriage, and ultimately gets you closer to the Lord. Remember, no matter how far the world gets from God and His goodness, you can know the truth and stay rooted in it for your life and marriage to be forever fruitful.

With my love and always for His glory,
Barbara Marcella

1

The Creation of Male and Female

In order to understand God's design and desire for marriage, we need to go back to the beginning, where it all began. Let's turn to the following verses in your Bible and read how God made the world, and ultimately man.

Genesis 1-3

We can see from verse **1:31** that everything that God originally made was very good. God gave Adam something to do: tend and rule over God's creation in the Garden of Eden, He even included Adam in the naming of all of the animals. But as we read further in verse **2:20**, we see that Adam did not find any of the animals to be compatible (a helper) with him. So God performs the very first surgery ever—In verses **2:21-23**, God places Adam in a deep sleep, takes one of his ribs, and alas, the woman is created.

How incredible it must have been to watch Adam see this beautiful woman made from his very own flesh—not exactly like him, but similar and yet different in all the perfect ways, being presented to him. God is a romantic, for sure.

Unfortunately, the story doesn't end there with a happily ever after. In **chapter 3, verses 1-6**, Eve is tempted by the serpent (Satan), disobeys the Lord, and commits the very first sin. She then gives the forbidden fruit to her husband and he eats it as well. Life will never be the same for them, and every person born thereafter.

In **verses 3:14–20**, we see the curse is placed on the serpent, the ground, and mankind. Man's work would now be filled with struggle and fatigue from having to provide for his wife and family. The woman would now bear children in pain, her husband would rule over her, and she would rely on him all the days of her life. Death, physically and spiritually, has also now entered the picture.

But God. God always has a plan far before we can think of the next step. He could have simply gotten rid of Adam and Eve, but He didn't. The story does not end here. In **verse 3:15**, we see a promise being made by God to all men of a future Savior coming:

And I will put enmity between thee and the woman, and between thy seed and her seed; it shall bruise thy head, and thou shalt bruise his heel. Genesis 3:15

1. Who does God create in **Genesis 1:27?**

2. On what day did God create man? **(Genesis 1:26-31)**

3. Why do you think God calls His creation "very good" instead of just "good" like the other times? **(Genesis 1:31)**

4. Why do you think Adam couldn't find a helper among all of the animals? What was similar about the woman; what was different?

5. What does it mean to you that you've been created in the image of God?

How amazing is it that you and I were created just like the Lord? None of Earth's creatures, including the plants and animals were created like Him. But we were! God created men and women with three parts just like Him:

a soul (the Father), a body (Jesus), and a spirit (the Holy Spirit):

And the Lord formed man of the dust of the ground, and breathed into his nostrils the breath of life; and man became a living soul. Genesis 2:7

God could've just left Adam and Eve as they were, living together and helping each other—but God did something even more amazing. He made them one flesh in marriage. God never does things without a purpose and a good reason behind it. Next, let's read about the first marriage and why it was so special to make this bond between the man and woman—and why it is still true and so important today.

2

The First Marriage

Therefore shall a man leave his father and mother, and shall cleave unto his wife: and they shall be one flesh. (Genesis 2:24)

B efore children, family, and government—marriage was the first institution created. The special relationship between a man and his wife is so intimate, so holy, and above all other earthly relationships, God went as far as declaring, "They shall be one flesh". In more ways than just physical, marriage brings two distinct souls together to share a life, create more life, and help each other through its many seasons. Let's turn to the following verses to learn about the first marriage and how holy and sacred it is to the Lord.

Genesis 2:24-25
Matthew 19:4-6
Mark 10: 6-9
Proverbs 18:22

Throughout these verses, we come to understand that the purpose of marriage is for companionship/a helper **(Genesis 2:18)** and it is to last a lifetime **(Mark 10:9, Romans 7:2, 1 Corinthians 7:10)**. We also understand that God created them male and female, just like we see the animals also had their own counterparts. When God brought the woman to Adam, he must have been stunned. Finally, someone just like him, yet so different. Someone that he could talk to and have a relationship with, someone that was made from his very own flesh. The more I think about it, the more I am amazed at how God knows us so well that he literally custom-made and created someone who would fit Adam perfectly.

So why marriage? Why couldn't they just live together in the garden as they were? Contrary to today's mindset that a couple could simply live together without being married and reap the benefits of marriage—we see that before anything else happened between Adam and Eve, God Himself joined them together in a holy relationship **(Genesis 2:24-25)**. Notice that God did not do this for the animals. Sure, they were male and female and could create life, but the aspect of having a helper, coming into a relationship, and becoming one flesh (both physically and spiritually) was only given to mankind.

This gives us the understanding that we are very different from animals. We have a soul; we have understanding, we have a conscience, we have the ability to feel and love—we are created in His very image. Therefore, God establishes marriage and blesses it as a formal union between a man and a woman, and at the start of their married lives, they become one.

The idea of a man leaving the family he grew up with and cleaving unto his wife **(Matthew 19:5-6)** quite literally means that he is strongly adhering to, clinging to, and holding onto this woman that he made a vow to before God. He is now willingly becoming one flesh with her in all aspects of life (spiritual, emotional, and physical), and they are no longer twain (two). Marriage beautifully represents and encapsulates Christ (the Groom) and His church (the Bride), which includes all those who have received Him as their Lord and Savior. Despite society's constant effort to lead others to define marriage as they please—true marriage will never change because the marriage between man and woman is a direct representation of believers and their Savior.

Next, we'll read more about how marriage is a picture of a believer's relationship to Christ.

1. In **(Genesis 2:22)**, God chose to create a woman out of man's rib, why do you think He chose that body part? What other significance could there be that the woman was taken out of the man's rib?

2. In **(Genesis 2:25)**, why do you think God mentions that the man and his wife were both naked and not ashamed? Do you think it was more than just the physical aspect of being naked?

3. God mentions in **(Mark 10:8-9)** that no man should separate what God has put together. What do you think this means?

4. Now that you've read about marriage from God's perspective and His very words, do you have a deeper understanding of who marriage is intended for? God is not the author of confusion, but rather clarity and perfection. The world will continue deceiving others about who can get married, but now you know the truth and can stand by it with His word.

3

Marriage: A Picture of Our Relationship to Christ

Wives, submit yourselves unto your own husbands, as unto the Lord. For the husband is the head of the wife, even as Christ is the head of the church: and he is the savior of the body. (Ephesians 5:22-23)

To understand the Gospel is to understand that marriage truly is God's story. It's the story of Jesus and redemption all throughout the Bible. It's the story of a God so loving that He created humanity, which continued to run off and worship other gods and idols—but He wouldn't give up on them. When God created marriage, it was foreshadowing what Jesus would do for His bride (the Church/Christ followers), sacrifice Himself for her (His very own body and blood) so that she could have the gift of eternal life with abundant forgiveness. What a beautiful love story indeed!

Isaiah 54:5-8
Isaiah 62:5
Ephesians 5:22-33

1 Peter 3:1-7
Revelation 19:7

Throughout scripture, we see this theme of redemption woven into all of the stories. Adam and Eve sin, and then God rather than destroying them, makes a promise of His redemption for all mankind in the future because He loves them. **(Genesis 3:15)** We read about God choosing His people (Israel) and them constantly disobeying, running from, and turning their hearts from Him. Then, when they've finally cried out to God, He redeems them and eventually   provides a way for all to be redeemed through His Son Jesus Christ. God is still very much   redeeming souls today.

The creation of marriage mirrors God's relationship with us (the church). Jesus is the head: (the husband, because Adam was created first) **(1 Timothy 2:13)**, and the Christians are the body: (the wife, Eve because she was created for Adam) **(1 Corinthians 11:9)**. The husband/groom being the head (like Jesus is), has the special role of loving his beloved wife and providing for her **(Ephesians 5:25)**. The wife/bride is to submit to her husband and his leadership because he is the head of their relationship **(Ephesians 5:22)**.

In the same way, God loves us, and we submit to Him. Jesus (God) left His home in heaven to be among us and die for our sins—the husband leaves his mother and father to cleave unto his wife when they get married and become one **(Ephesians 5:31)**.

Eve was created from Adam's side— his rib. In the same way, when Jesus was on the cross, He was pierced from His side, and His bride (the church) was redeemed from the sacrificial flow of blood and water that came out of Him **(John 19:34, Ephesians 5:25-26)**. It really is incredible once you understand what even the apostle Paul (the writer of most of the New Testament) considered a great mystery, and how God designed marriage exactly like His love for us **(Ephesians 5:32)**.

This is why there is no other marriage apart from the one God created: between one man and one woman.

A self-sacrificing and unconditional love that redeems and forgives over and over again. No one really gives it much thought, but there is a reason why everyone is anticipating the arrival of the beautiful bride at weddings. She is the picture of purity in a white dress: adorned, spotless, and simply beautiful for her husband, who is waiting for her at the altar. **(Ephesians 5:27)**

God gave the gift of marriage to the world to point to the Gospel. Christians who live out their marriages in faith, love, and forgiveness shine as lights and reflect the character and loving nature of their Creator.

"... there is no other marriage apart from
the ... created between one man and one
woman.

4

Husband and Wife Unique Roles

Just like God created male and female distinctly, He also gave them very unique roles that would complement each other in the life they would share together. Men are to be the head of the family as leaders and women, being the weaker vessel, created after and for the man, are to submit to the leadership of their husband.

As a direct representation of Jesus (the man) and His Church (the woman), the roles are quite easy to understand. Jesus loves and takes care of His followers and His followers submit to Him willingly because they know and trust that He will take care of them. Marriage perfectly depicts this beautiful relationship.

Genesis 3:16
Proverbs 31:27
1 Corinthians 11:3
1 Corinthians 11:11
Ephesians 5:22-33

Colossians 3:18-20
Titus 2:3-5
1 Peter 3:1-7

God gives the husband the important responsibility of loving his wife, being the leader, provider, and protector of his household. The husband essentially gives himself, sacrificially, for his wife and loves and respects her all the days of his life (just like Jesus gave Himself for us) **(Ephesians 5:23-25)**.

The woman has the important role of submitting, loving, and respecting the leadership of her husband, having children, teaching them, taking care of her household, being a keeper of the home, and, when she is older, to be an example and teacher to the younger women **(Ephesians 5:22, Proverbs 31:27, Titus 2:3-5)**.

Both the husband and wife have the responsibility of loving and submitting to one another out of their deep respect for Jesus **(Ephesians 5:21)**. It's a two-way street that God made to work perfectly in unison. But society has twisted this beautiful partnership throughout the years and given it a negative view. But if you know God's character and understand His word, you know that God does all things for our good and His glory **(Romans 8:28, Isaiah 43:7)**.

Many women today view submission as a bad term. But the truth is, when a man loves his wife the way God instructs him to, and he steps into his role as a leader and provider—caring, loving, cherishing, and respecting his wife and family, the wife will happily submit to him because she knows he loves her and will take care of her. Similarly, as time went on, many men did not listen to God's instruction, and took advantage of being the head of their wives and families, mistreating the very ones they were entrusted with loving and caring for. Therefore, because of this, we saw a shift in roles over time, as women decided to take on the role of providing so that they perhaps could escape the harsh treatment and neglect of their husbands and could live a better life in peace.

But sadly, both of these views are wrong because they are not the roles God intended for marriage.

No family is perfect, and every situation is different, but the Lord sees and knows each one. God has given us the freedom to choose how to live our lives, but He's also given us His instructions in his word. So whether we choose to honor God despite our circumstances is up to us.

If we choose to follow the Lord's path and His righteous way of living, He will bless us and our loved ones, and we will be a light for others to see in a world so riddled with darkness.

1. What are some responsibilities of the husband? **(Ephesians 5:23, 1 Peter 3:7)**

2. What are some responsibilities of the wife? **(Ephesians 5:22, Proverbs 31:27)**

3. What are some responsibilities for both the husband and wife? **(Ephesians 5:21)**

4. Is this view very different than the one that society has taught you? How so?

5

Love never fails-- Do you pass the test?

And now abideth faith, hope, charity, these three; but the greatest of these is charity. ~1 Corinthians 13:13

(1 Corinthians 13:4-13)

Y ou probably recognize these verses from a wedding you have been to. It is one of the most popular verses to recite during the ceremony. To give you some context, it was a letter that the apostle Paul sent to the church (Christian believers) that was located in Corinth (modern-day Greece). He wrote to them regarding how those who were a new creation in Christ were now to live their lives in such a way that glorified their Lord Jesus Christ, while also uplifting one another and being a light to the world living in darkness around them.

It's understandable why these verses would apply to a new marriage. It describes how charity (the quality one should possess towards another person) has all of these beautiful attributes such as patience, kindness, forgiveness, selflessness, etc... and how we should act towards the one we vow our lives to.

It's also the very characteristics the Lord has towards us. He was willing to lay down His very life for us, even though we don't deserve anything. It's unconditional love that He modeled for us, He was the very example, and if we say we are His followers, we should also model that love first in our marriages.

1. Now I have a little exercise for you to try out. As you read over **1 Corinthians 13:4-8**, Whenever it says the word charity, replace it with your name. Now read it, do your actions and attitude align with the verses?

It's okay if they don't, I failed miserably too. Jesus understands that no one is perfect, that's why He died for us, because He is! But these verses are something we should use to hold ourselves accountable so that we may grow every day and get better at loving our spouses and others like Jesus does. Remember, love isn't a feeling, but a choice we get to make every day.

6

Marriage and Intimacy

Marriage is honorable in all, and the bed undefiled: but whoremongers and adulterers God will judge. (Hebrews 13:4)

S atan has long been perverting and attacking what God intended as a beautiful and intimate gift within marriage. God's original design for sex between a husband and his wife was perfect, pure, and good. Today, we see a culture that is sex-driven with no thought or care about the consequences that derive from this act. But the Lord makes it clear that whoever engages in sex outside of marriage commits a sin not only against the Lord but their own body **(1 Corinthians 6:18).**

God gave sex as a gift between a husband and his wife to enjoy within the parameters of marriage, and the gift that comes out of that intimate love is children. **The Book of Song of Solomon** in the Bible poetically expresses the beauty of intimate love between a husband and wife within marriage.

Genesis 2:24
Genesis 4:1
Song of Solomon

1 Thessalonians 4:3-4
Hebrews 13:4
1 Corinthians 6:9-11
1 Corinthians 7:1-9

Once Adam and Eve were married, the Bible tells us they came together, and Adam knew his wife, and she conceived **(Genesis 4:1).**

Notice that God didn't mention them being intimate until *after* He married them. Mankind wasn't like the animals that could simply have sex without a thought solely to procreate. There was something deeper here. Mankind was created in God's very own image. Therefore they will be held accountable, and God has set a day in which He will judge how they've chosen to live in them. This is especially the case for Christians, whose bodies are revealed to be the temple of the Holy Spirit in the Bible **(1 Corinthians 6:18-20).**

Our world continues to deceive many through movies, shows, and books of people having "casual sex", relationships normalizing moving in together, traveling, and living as a married couple without the commitment of marriage, music idolizing immoral sex, and the list goes on and on. But contrary to the world's modern thinking, God's word and standards stay the same **(Hebrews 13:8).**

What was a sin 2,000 years ago is still very much a sin today.

Satan is very sneaky in his tactics because he hates mankind and wants to destroy what God made good. When you're not married, he does everything to tempt you to have sex.

But when you are married and free to enjoy sex—he does everything to pull you apart.

This is the reason Paul emphasizes, in **1 Corinthians 7,** the importance of couples marrying if they are tempted to sexually sin. He tells married couples to come together frequently within their relationship so that Satan does not have a chance to tempt them to sexually sin outside of marriage.

God does not place boundaries on something so important because He wants to "ruin our fun," but on the contrary, He wants to protect us from getting hurt.

So many lives are ruined because of sexual sin. There is no such thing as "casual sex" because after being intimate with someone, that scar is forever left behind.

In **John 8:1-11,** we read the story of a woman who is caught in the act of adultery, and the Scribes and Pharisees take her to Jesus. In the law of Moses, the consequence of adultery was death by stoning. Jesus instead says, *He that is without sin among you, let him cast the first stone at her.*

One by one, they all drop the stones and leave her behind with Jesus. Jesus then looks at her and tells her He doesn't condemn her and to go and sin no more. This story brings me to tears. Jesus had so much compassion for her. He knew she was guilty of death for what she did—but instead of the punishment that she deserved, He forgave her and told her to sin no more. She was free to change her life around and stop this sinful and destructive life she was living. That's what repentance is friends.

No one is perfect. We are all sinners, and that is why Jesus had to die on the cross for every one of us. If you are currently living in sexual sin or have done so in the past, please know that you can repent of it, stop doing it, and change your life. You can be forgiven and be set free. You are no longer bound by the chains of sin once you accept Christ as your Savior, His blood paid for it all. You can be made a new creature—the old things have passed away, and you are free to live a new life. You are no longer a prisoner of your past! **(2 Corinthians 5:17)**

7

Teaching on Divorce

He saith unto them, Moses because of the
hardness of your hearts suffered you to put away
your wives: but from the beginning it was not so.
(Matthew 19:8)

When a joyous couple is declaring their vows to one another in front of loved ones on their wedding day, you would never even think of the possibility of divorce on the horizon. But sadly, this is a reality that is occurring more frequently than we'd like to admit.

Divorce affects more than just the husband and wife in the relationship. Sadly, children, friendships, family, and other relationships suffer as well when a marriage ends. When the Pharisees asked Jesus about divorce and if it was lawful to put away your wife for every cause, Jesus had an answer. He stated that during Moses' time, the people had hardened their hearts so much that the Lord finally gave them what they wanted: divorce. But from the beginning, it was never God's intention.

Malachi 2:16
Matthew 5:31-32

Matthew 19:1-9
Mark 10:2-12
Luke 16:18
Romans 7:2-3
1 Corinthians 7:10-17
1 Corinthians 7:39
Hebrews 13:4

From the beginning, the Lord always intended for a husband and wife to stay together as the saying goes, "until death do us part". It is a vow we make when we get married, and God does not take it lightly. Since marriage is a representation of our relationship with Jesus, it makes sense that God would want reconciliation and forgiveness between a couple, rather than complete separation.

There is one case that Jesus mentions in which God allows for divorce, and that is the infidelity of one spouse **(Matthew 5:31-32)**. But even in difficult situations, if possible, God would prefer forgiveness and breathing new life into a marriage.

In cases where a spouse passes away, the widower is no longer bound by marriage and is free to be married once again **(1 Corinthians 7:39).**

Sadly, we do live in a broken world, but God is still merciful. Sometimes things just don't work out the way we wanted, whether that be with our own marriage or perhaps we didn't have the best example from our parents. God can still meet you where you are, forgive you, and help you make things right so that you can live righteously for the Lord and reap the blessings He has in store. After all, God is the ultimate redeemer.

8
Proverbs 31: The Virtuous Woman

Favour is deceitful, and beauty is vain: but a woman that feareth the Lord, she shall be praised. (Proverbs 31:30)

Proverbs 18:22
Proverbs 31:10-31
1 Peter 3:1-6

The book of Proverbs in the Old Testament is written by the son of King David, King Solomon. He was given wisdom and understanding from the Lord that was unmatched even to this day. The Lord was so pleased with Solomon's humble request that He also granted him riches and honor and promised him a long life if he walked in His ways and kept the Lord's commandments all of his life **(1 Kings 3:3-15).**

At the end of the book of Proverbs, in chapter 31 starting at verse 10 we have this beautiful description of what the character of a virtuous woman looks like. This type of woman has strength and wisdom that doesn't come from the world—rather, she obtains her strength, beauty, and worth from the Lord.

Considering that Solomon was the wisest man to live and that he received his wisdom from the Lord, I would say this description is something to strive for as a woman. Her price is far above rubies and any man who finds her as a wife surely will be blessed and obtain favor from the Lord.

Wherever you look, women today are mostly portrayed as being strong, independent, and not needing a man to help them achieve what they want. They can do it all on their own, and they're not afraid to speak their mind.

But is that really the character that God intended for women?

From the beginning, we saw that the woman was the weaker vessel of the two **(1 Peter 3:7)**, but that doesn't necessarily mean weak in character and spirit. It doesn't mean weak in a negative sense; rather, it just means that the woman was created for the man, and he was to look after her and take care of her.

Quite obviously and scientifically, it is a fact that, in most cases, a man is physically (bodily) stronger than a woman. But since a woman was created as a helper to the man, God gave her unique attributes that would complement the man. **Inner strength in the form of her spirit and character.**

Sometimes, though, husbands aren't the spiritual heads that God intended them to be. Even so, wives are instructed to continue to submit to them as unto God. Actions are far more important than words, and the simple act of doing the right thing in God's eyes—may one day be the very example and thing that will lead them to the Lord **(1 Peter 3:1).**

Did you ever stop and think about why, in most cases, a little child calls out to their mommy when they are sad, scared, hurt, or need to be comforted? Women have this gentleness that God gave them in order to love others in this manner. Men love too, but it's very different than the special way a woman does.

It's simply built into the way we're created. It makes sense that God wouldn't make someone exactly like Adam with the same strengths and weaknesses, but rather someone that is stronger in other areas that he is not, and has weaknesses where he has strengths. A balance to work together as a team, in perfect unison. **(1 Peter 3:7)**

Contrary to modern thinking, a woman with a gentle spirit that is rooted in the Lord, is a woman who is strong and will not be shaken.

Rather than trying to become women that fit the media's mold and idea of what a woman is—let's aspire to be women of integrity after God's own heart so that we could be the type of women our husbands need to grow, thrive, and be the leaders God intended them to be!

1. What kind of skills do we see the virtuous woman have in **Proverbs 31:13-19**? Do you think you have any of these skills? Which skills would you like to learn so you could apply them to your life?

2. In verse 30, we read how favour is deceitful and beauty is vain. As a woman, it can be difficult not to think about beauty, especially when comparing ourselves with other women. Is this something that affects you? What are ways you can have a positive attitude about your life without having to focus too much on physical beauty? (Whatever age you are.) Remember, God made

you beautiful in every aspect, and there is beauty in every season of our lives.

3. The last verse of the Proverbs chapter **(31:31)** ends with "let her own works praise her in the gates". What do you think this means? In today's media, we see a lot of self-praise being put on display. What kind of praise does the Lord prefer for us?

9

Praying Over Your Marriage

Confess your faults one to another, and pray one for another, that ye may be healed. The effectual fervent prayer of a righteous man availeth much.
~James 5:16

We now have the privilege of being able to go directly to God with our requests, and He certainly wants us to! I can't stress enough how important and life-giving praying over our marriage is. The most difficult and seemingly impossible situations become possible with the God of the impossible. Our marriages and husbands need to be protected at all costs from the enemy (Satan) that wants to attack it and see it fail. Fill your marriage with prayer, and God will bless you and protect you all the days of your lives, and when troubles do arise (because they will), you will stand upon the firm foundation of Jesus Christ.

Even before you have a husband, pray for him! I know it's kind of odd to do, but God instructs us to pray at all times. At the very beginning of your marriage, build it on a firm foundation upon the rock of Jesus **(Matthew 7:24-27)**. Even if you never did, it is never too late to start! Below are just a few things you can start to pray over for your marriage and husband.

His faith and salvation: pray that the Lord opens up His heart and mind to Him and He comes to trust in Jesus as His personal Savior. **(Psalm 18:2-3)**

His health: pray that the Lord keeps him healthy and strong to provide for his family all the days of his life. **(Isaiah 53:5)**

His mind: pray that God guards his heart and mind and that he meditates on His word all the days of his life. **(Psalm 1:2)**

His temptations: pray that the Lord keeps him strong against temptation and keeps his eyes and heart fixed on Him and your marriage. **(1 Corinthians 10:13)**

His job/work: pray that he works honestly with integrity and does well at his workplace. **(Proverbs 22:29)**

His leadership: pray that he can be a godly husband and father to his family. **(1 Peter 3:7)**

His protection: pray that the Lord keeps him safe from all evil. **(Psalm 91:1)**

His sexuality: pray that the Lord guards his heart and mind and that he has the strength to flee sexual immorality. **(1 Corinthians 6:18-20)**

His wisdom in life/finances: pray that the Lord gives him the wisdom to make the right decisions to lead his family. **(Philippians 4:19)**

His trials: pray that the Lord gives him the strength to get through all of life's troubles. **(1 Peter 1:6-7)**

His priorities: pray that he prioritizes the Lord first and his family before all things. **(Matthew 6:33)**

His fatherhood: pray that he loves and leads His children in the admonition of God. **(Ephesians 6:4)**

His fears: pray over his anxieties, worries, and fears. Perfect love casts out all fear pray that the Lord will comfort Him. **(Joshua 1:9)**

His purpose: pray that the Lord helps him find his purpose in Him and he grows with all of the skills and talents he has been given to become all that God has called him to be. **(2 Thessalonians 1:11-12)**

His relationships: pray that God surrounds him with godly relationships that encourage him to be a godly man. **(Proverbs 13:20)**

His wife: you need prayer as well! Pray that you become the godly wife your husband needs. A wife who loves, cherishes, respects, honors, and submits to his leadership so that you can dwell in unity. **(Ephesians 5:22)**

Your marriage: pray for unity in your marriage and that your hearts be bound together as one. Pray that you both honor, love, and respect each other all the days of your lives. In the bad, good, and mundane seasons that come your way, pray that you always go to the Lord first. Pray that your marriage bed is kept pure and that you only have eyes for one another. Pray that your marriage will be a testimony of God's endless love for humanity and that it glorifies Him. Pray that your marriage is a light to others around you and leaves a legacy of faith.

We often overlook prayer, but God tells us that the prayers of a righteous person (one whose heart is right with the Lord) are effective and powerful **(James 5:16)**. God can do the impossible in your life and marriage. Go to Him with all of your needs and thank Him for all that He has already done. Make prayer the first thing you do before all else.

10
Better Together

Two are better than one; because they have a good reward for their labour. For if they fall, the one will lift up his fellow: but woe to him that is alone when he falleth: for he hath not another to help him. ~Ecclesiastes 4:9-10

Proverbs 27:17
Amos 3:3
Romans 15:1
Galatians 6:2
Philippians 2:3-4
1 Peter 4:8-10
2 Corinthians 6:14-18

For the past few years, I've been researching and gaining interest in natural health. Through my studies, I've also learned that when certain plants or herbs are taken together—their potency and healing abilities become even stronger than if taken alone. The same idea applies to marriage. If it wasn't so, God wouldn't have created Eve as a wife and helper for Adam. He would've just left him alone to dwell in the garden with the animals. But everything God creates is good as we've learned in the first chapter— and He has a grand purpose and intended beauty for it all.

Sadly through the years, marriage has been portrayed in a negative light. Other than the excitement of the wedding day itself, oftentimes marriage is viewed as an end to life rather than a beginning. From hearing the complaints of older generations and the way the media portrayed marriage— I myself grew up thinking that once I got married, my life would be "over". The end of all fun and freedom. The end of my hopes and dreams. Based on some conversations I had heard, marriage felt like a ball and chain would be placed on my feet.

But I'm here to tell you that none of that is true. For me, marriage was the beginning and freedom from all of that weight.

Yes, marriage is indeed the end of certain things. It's the end of singleness and casual dating. It's the end of breaking up or not knowing whether the relationship will go anywhere. It's the end of a selfish lifestyle.

But marriage is the beginning of so many good things. It's the beginning of a commitment that no matter the circumstances—your spouse will love you unconditionally. It's the beginning of sharing life's moments, ups, downs, and everything in between— together. It's the beginning of freedom in the gift of intimacy that God gave between a husband and wife—free of shame.

Marriage helps you mature and grow in ways you wouldn't be able to if you stayed single. Sure, dating is fun— but that's all it is. You don't know if the other person will decide to leave one day—and sadly that does happen, because there is no commitment. But in marriage, you are set free in Christ from all of that.

There is security in a Christ-centered (God-focused marriage), it gives you a strong foundation to work through all of the bumps and gives you strength to get you through the difficult times.

But for a Christ-centered marriage to happen— God also instructs us to not be unequally yoked with unbelievers **(2 Corinthians 6:14-18)**. This also applies to close relationships, but most importantly to marriage. It's not that God doesn't want us to be respectful and loving to others, He does because remember we are all created in His image **(Genesis 1:27)**—but becoming one with a person who does not believe in Christ is not wise. The reason is that the unbeliever can often turn the other person away from Christ with their foreign beliefs and traditions. It can also hinder your growth and sanctification (meaning slow down the process of God making you holy and perfect like Him through the trials and circumstances we face in life.)

Imagine a pair of oxen yoked together (a wooden bar that joins them together by their necks)— when they begin to walk forward, they are linked so they naturally go in the same direction. But, if one decides to turn a different way than the other— well it will throw everything off and it make it quite difficult for them to keep walking together, if not impossible. The same principle applies to marriage.

God specifically states that there is no communion between the light and darkness. He calls us to be separate from them. Even Solomon with all of his wisdom, had his heart turned away from the Lord when He disobeyed God and married women from foreign lands with strange gods **(1 Kings 11:4)**.

Even so, if you have married someone with different beliefs, I believe God can restore any relationship to Himself, no matter what comes between. The truth is when you center your relationship on Christ, you can have a vibrant and fruitful marriage. God unites two imperfect people in marriage so that He can sharpen, purify, and sanctify them **(Proverbs 27:17).**

No, it won't be perfect, but the God you place your trust in is. And He will carry you through all of life's storms and you'll come out stronger on the other side of it—together. That's why a Christian marriage is made up of three— one husband, one wife, and Jesus in the center. Even with the most difficult circumstances, that's a solid foundation that will be hard to break **(Ecclesiastes 4:12, Matthew 7:24-25).**

11
Final Words

And we know that all things work together for good to them that love God, to them who are the called according to his purpose ~ Romans 8:28

I can still remember the moment my husband and I were pronounced husband and wife like it was just yesterday. A little over two years ago to be exact. We still didn't have a set place to live, but in that long-awaited moment, everything was made new. Technically our wedding in the summer of 2021 falls under the category of the pandemic couples. But judging from our wedding day—you would never know it.

Throughout the entire two years of planning, everything was unknown and the situation seemed to worsen day by day. I lost my beloved *Nonno* (grandfather), and I won't lie and say I didn't cry every time I photographed a wedding with masks on. But in the midst of it all, we prayed over our wedding day and every single detail about it. We decided to stay with the date, trusting that the Lord would work it out for our good and His glory. I realized that no matter how impossible a situation seemed— if I truly believed the words of God like I said I did, then I needed to believe that He could make the impossible possible.

And the impossible God did. One month before our wedding day, all the mandates were lifted. No masks, no limit on guests, no indoor restrictions.

When I woke up on the day of our wedding and saw the glorious sun shining inside my bedroom window, I was overwhelmed with joy. I didn't cry a single tear that day because I was so overjoyed with what God had done for us.

And I didn't deserve any of it. As silly and vain as a wedding day seems to worry that much over, God's unending love and grace surpassed all of our prayers. Two years later I still love to recount and give glory to God for all that He did. This bible study serves as a way to honor the Lord for all that He provided and still continues to do so today. I pray that this study has brought you more understanding of God's beautiful plan and intention for marriage.

All this to say, I am no expert in marriage— but I trust a God that is. Yes, it's true that marriage is hard work, but anything worth it is. Please know that no marriage is without its flaws. We can have the most wonderful husband or be the most incredible wife— but still fall short. God never intended us to depend on our spouses to fulfill the desire only He could. We will set ourselves up for disappointment if we fail to realize that no matter how amazing a person can be, they, like us, are only human. Our spouses are no substitute for the Lord, for only He was meant to fill the void that lies within all of our hearts.

Ladies, I pray you never compromise until the Lord brings you the man who is worthy of you and loves you (almost as much) as Jesus does. I hope that in the waiting you trust in His goodness and become the virtuous woman filled with integrity and righteousness after God's own heart—the wife that your future husband is searching for. I'm just an ordinary girl, with an extraordinary God that went above and beyond to save me and you. I pray most of all that this study blesses you and that you come to know the God who loves you without end.

With my love and always for His glory,
Barbara Marcella

12

The Gospel

I 'm so grateful that you are here and made time to read through this study! I poured my heart and mind into it having dedicated countless hours studying and praying that these words would be a reflection of God's purpose for marriage. If you don't know Jesus Christ as your personal Lord and Savior, I'd like to invite you to come into His presence and receive His good gift of salvation. From the beginning, God had a perfect plan, but once Adam and Eve sinned, mankind would never be the same. Both physical and spiritual death came into the picture that day.

God's word in the Bible tells us that there is no one who is righteous or good **(Romans 3:10)**.

We have all turned from God and sinned against the very One who created us **(Romans 3:11-12)**.

We are all sinners who come short of the glory of God, our sin separates us from Him and we therefore cannot be in His holy and perfect presence **(Romans 3:23)**.

No amount of "good" that we do can save us **(Ephesians 2:8-9)**.

Going to church can't save us. Religion and traditions can't save us **(Mark 7:5-13)**.

But God in all of His goodness, mercy, love, and grace manifested in the flesh as the Son of God (Jesus) was born of a virgin and lived a holy, sinless life, died on the cross, shed His innocent blood and washed us of our sins— and three days later rose again and lives today, seated at the right hand of God. He gave Himself as the ultimate sacrifice so that one day we could live eternally with Him in His glorious presence. What an incredible free gift! **(John 3:16)**

God was willing to take our place on the cross, taking our deserving punishment, that if we would choose to trust Him as our Savior, we wouldn't be eternally separated from him in Hell, but would live forever in glory with Him.

Friend, if you don't know Jesus as your Savior, no amount of religious rituals and traditions, "being a good person" could save you, you are already condemned **(John 3:18).**

But if you are reading this, you still have time to accept His wonderful gift of life and know that He has a purpose for you.

Admit that you, like all people, are a sinner **(Romans 3:23).**

Believe in what Jesus did on the cross for you—He shed His blood, died, and three days later defeated death and rose again **(Romans 5:8-11).**

Call upon the Lord and ask Him to come into your heart and save you **(Romans 10:13).**

Repent of all your sins and ask God to forgive you **(Acts 3:19).**

The moment you receive the Lord, you have God's promise of eternal life and have been born again which Jesus reveals you must do in order to be saved **(John 3:1-7).**

God loves you and wants you to come to know Him! If you are alive, there's still time for you— you can accept God's gift of salvation and know your eternity is secure. But don't wait to make this decision, for time is not promised to anyone **(James 4:13-15, 2 Corinthians 6:2).** Jesus can come at any moment for His bride (Christian believers) **(Matthew 24:42).** He has so much more in store for you—more than anything you leave behind. He can do the impossible in your life and give you a new one with a beautiful purpose. Trust in Him and all of His goodness. I promise you it will be the greatest decision you will ever make.

About the Author

Barbara Marcella is a photographer but when she's not behind the camera, you can find her nestled between the books, at the local library where she works.

As a newly-wed wife, she loves to spend time in the kitchen cooking up delicious meals for her husband who never ceases with his shenanigans but always succeeds in putting a smile on her face. Barbara is passionate about encouraging women to live the way God intended as revealed in His word.

She believes the Bible to be the word of God and the greatest source of instruction a Christian can follow. She sees God's hands woven through every season of her life and loves to share it with others in hopes that they too may see the goodness of God in their lives.

You can find Barbara and more of her creative work at:
www.barbaramarcellablog.com

www.ingramcontent.com/pod-product-compliance
Lightning Source LLC
Chambersburg PA
CBHW071739020426
42331CB00008B/2091